Walking in the Overflow

Living a Life of Abundance by Believing
What God Can Do

Scott L. Gordon

Foreword by Dr. G. Calvin McCutchen

Published by Book Writing Genie
Cover design by Book Writing Genie
ISBN: Printed in the United States

If you would like to contact me, or for additional
Copies send to:
Calvary Baptist Church
412 North 7th Street
Sapulpa, Oklahoma 74066-3041
918-224-1167

Book Writing Genie

Contents:

Dedication:

First and foremost, I would like to thank God, who is head of my life. To my wife Kristi, who has been there with love and has been a source of inspiration and a motivator as we walk in the overflow; to my children Brandon, Nastosha, and Taylor; to my grandparents, both of my parents' mothers, Fairella and Louise; to my mother Johnnie Mae and father Arthur Lee; to my uncle Jerry and aunt Ida Bell Mclaurin; and to my other grandparents, Morgan Austin, John and Dorothy Pruitt who, along with Ida Bell, went on to be with the Lord.

To my Pastor Dr. G. Calvin and Adelene McCutchen, who have been a blessing to my wife and I. Dr McCutchen is a pastor, friend, and one of the greatest role models a pastor can have.

To my church family, Calvary Baptist Church in Sapulpa, Oklahoma, who has definitely been a blessing to me and my family, and all the mothers of the church and the pastoral staff who keep me in prayer, special thanks to Kristi Roe Owens for the excellent proofreading in this manuscript

Section 1: Walking in the Overflow

Foreword by
Dr. G. Calvin McCutchen, Sr.

Many people are not moving with God today sim- ply because they are not willing to take the small steps He placed before them.

Don't be afraid to take small steps. The Bible promises us that if we are faithful in small matters, one day – we will be rulers over many larger things.

The impossible, many times, is just simply the untried. We should all learn to grow wherever we're planted.

All great discoveries have been made by people whose faith ran ahead of their minds.

As believers we need to learn to stretch, to reach out where God is. Always aim high and take risks. Don't become so caught up in small matters that you can't take advantage of important opportunities. Never be guilty of letting down your bucket into an empty well.

Dream big. Reach the full potential of your calling. I have examined the manuscript of Pastor Gordon's Book – Walking In The Overflow. He is careful to give God all the credit for the blessings He has bestowed upon him as a beginning Pastor of a growing church.

He followed his successor, Reverend Ervin Ruth, as Joshua followed Moses. Making a difference in today's world never just happens; it is always a result of faith com- bined with works. Never be guilty of running around with a spiritual cup only half full.

God has all kinds of blessings for us – with our names on it. Remember as you read this book – no problem is too large for God's intervention and no person is too small for God's attention. Follow God – take no chance of getting lost. If Jesus can't take you to the top – no one else will.

One of the Whosoevers,

G. Calvin McCutchen, Sr., Pastor Mt. Zion Baptist Church Tulsa, OK

Chapter 1:

Walking in the Overflow

As pastor of one of the greatest churches in the world, Calvary Baptist Church in Sapulpa,

Oklahoma, as we have just started a new year I was led to write on the subject of "walking in the overflow." I am blessed be- cause at this time in my life I am being tried on every side, but because God said it, I can do it. In Joshua chapter one, there is a great outline, It's really simple. In verses 1-9, God is speaking to Joshua. In verses 10-15, Joshua then turns to the people and speaks to the children of Israel. And in verses 16-18, the people reply back to Joshua. It's simple to outline just by who is speaking and to whom they're speak- ing. As I look at verses 1-9 and look at how God prepared Joshua to enter into the land, I pray it will help you walk in the overflow. The whole book of Joshua, particularly the first five chapters, is just a preparation for entering into the land. You have to make preparation to enter into the over- flow; they don't enter in to fight the battle of Jericho until chapter 6. So throughout the first five chapters they are preparing, laying some ground work. As a Christian, I have learned it is important to have a foundation built on Jesus Christ. I have been living my life to the fullest for the past 11 years. It has not been easy, but I have learned if God is for you, it doesn't matter who is against you. It says in verses 1-9:

1After the death of Moses the LORD's servant, the LORD spoke to Joshua son of Nun, Moses' assistant. He said,

2"Now that my servant Moses is dead, you must lead my people across the Jordan River into the land I am giving them.

3I promise you what I promised Moses: 'everywhere you go, you will be on land I have given you—

4from the Negev Desert in the south to the Lebanon mountains in the north, from the Euphrates River on the east to the Mediterranean Sea on the west, and all the land of the Hittites.'

5No one will be able to stand their ground against you as long as you live. For I will be with you as I was with Moses. I will not fail you or abandon you.

6"Be strong and courageous, for you will lead my people to possess all the land I swore to give their ancestors.

7Be strong and very courageous. Obey all the laws Moses gave you. Do not turn away from them, and you will be suc- cessful in everything you do.

8Study this Book of the Law continually. Meditate on it day and night so you may be sure to obey all that is written in it. Only then will you succeed. 9I command you—be strong and courageous! Do not be afraid or discouraged. For the LORD your God is with you wherever you go."

In the first nine verses of Joshua chapter 1, I find a few principles that I need as groundwork as we begin to walk into the overflow. Faith takes the land. It's faith and faith alone. But there are ways that God builds faith. we know that the beginning of Joshua takes place after the death of Moses. Moses died at a ripe old age of 120 years old. I learned from Joshua 24:29 that Joshua was 110 years old at his death. Through a process of mathematics, in the book of Joshua there was a seven year war over the land that took place with the Israelites. And there were approximately 23 years of occupation and possessing and dividing out as the Israelites inheritance walking in the overflow before Joshua passes off the scene. Joshua was about 80 years old when he went in to take the land.

Now I don't know about you, but when I think about Joshua and the battle of Jericho and all those things I learned in B T U & Sunday school, I don't think about an 80-year-old man. I've always pictured Joshua as a younger man, maybe my age, 37-year-old. I just didn't picture him as an 80-year-old guy going in to do all these battles and fighting. It's not that you have to wait until you're 80 to enter into the land, but life prepares you to enter into the land. All of life prepares you to enter into the land.

I have learned God is able to fight the battle. It isn't easy being still; I question God and His answer is merely, "Be still and know I am God." I am learning all the twists and the turns that life takes, preparing us to enter the land. God is doing a work in our hearts. He's a sovereign God, and He controls all the circumstances, and He builds what He wants. He's doing a work. And it's the processes of life that prepare you to enter into the land. He has a plan for your life, and that plan is to be conformed to the image of His Son. He's working it out.

What did Joshua do to prepare himself to enter the land? He lived. He lived eighty years. He was born in the land of Egypt, he saw the great Exodus, and He saw all the plagues that God worked. He spent 40 years wandering in the wilderness, and a lot of things happened. As he did all these things, God was working on him. God was working in his life. A lot of us have the idea sometimes that in order to be used by God, in order to be a preacher, to be a pastor, to be a great evangelist, that we need to go to Bible school, we need to go to Bible college, we need all of these things. Don't get me wrong, I'm not down on Bible College—I went. But

I can tell you that most of my learning did not take place in the classroom. It didn't. It takes place as I live daily with people who had different ideas from different backgrounds. And as we had our ideas on the Bible intellec- tually challenged that prepared me more than the classes I took. Getting out of college and working in the world and rubbing shoulders with different people has prepared me more than any course I ever took in college. I never took a course on teaching the kids that I teach. I'm not sure that any kind of course would prepare you for that. You just have to kind of do it and learn to duck quickly.

Joshua learned to lead by following. He followed Mo- ses around for 40 years in the wilderness; you can imagine some of the scenes in Joshua's life. Twelve spies were sent out to stake out the land. They went throughout the land and then they came back and they gave a report. The major- ity, ten of them, gave a fearful report. They said, "the land is beautiful, yes, but there are giants." the problem is there, it just depends on how you look at it. With faith you can walk in the overflow; there are walled cities, there are all kinds of obstacles, and there is no way. We can't take it. I am re- minded that when Pastor Ervin Ruth died former pastor of Calvary, when I was appointed as Senior Pastor there were many who said I was too young. Some even left, but thank God there were many that had faith that God was able to help us walk in the overflow.

Chapter One: Walking in the Overflow

In the word of God, Joshua and his friend Caleb came back and said, "Their report is right, the land is beautiful, it's great, but God said He gave it to us; let's go in and take it." And the people picked up stones and were ready to stone Joshua. They picked up stones, they had them in their hands, and Joshua was thinking, "Okay, here I am, I'm mak- ing a stand for God and they're going to kill me." You may have taken a stand and stones are coming at you; stand still and know God, for He is your shield. The Word says that a "Shechaniah glory cloud came down on the tented meet- ing and the people dropped stones and scattered." Do you think Joshua learned something from that? Think about it. Here he is making a stand for God, making a strong stand. People pick up stones and get ready to stone him, and he's thinking, "This is it, it's over. I'll never get into the land." Then all of a sudden, God comes down and scatters every- body.

Yet another time Joshua learned something was in the valley of Rephidim, when he was down in the valley and fighting the battle and Moses was up on the hilltop, holding up the rod of God. And as his hands started to come down, they started to lose the battle. Aaron and Hur propped him up and held up his hands. Joshua learned something that day. He learned the battle is not his. The battle is God's. You may be in a battle, but just stand still and see God: "Lift Jesus us." The race is not given to the swift. You have to have faith if you get that idea that you can't do it, you can't take the land. There is just no way. It's just too much. But you've got the key to the front door. You've got to come to that point in your life where you have to walk by faith and stop claiming there's just no way and you can't do it. God is working in each one of our lives. He's bringing us to that point where we finally say, "I can do all things through Christ who strengthens me." Throw up your hands because God says, "You're all right; follow me."

It's life and all of life and its twists and it turns that you take that prepares you to enter into the land. This is walking in the overflow. When times get hard and it seems like I want to give up, God always shows up. Joshua 1:1-2 says, "Now after the death of Moses the servant of the LORD it came to pass, that the Lord spake unto Joshua the son of Nun, Moses' minister, saying, Moses my servant is dead..." Now think about that. Think about what Moses meant to these Jews. He was the man who came in when they were in bondage in Egypt, the man who was instrumental in lead- ing them out, the man who brought about the ten plagues. He was the man who went up on Mt. Sinai and talked with God face to face and then brought back the Command- ments. He wandered through the wilderness with them and brought water from a rock; all of these things Moses did were held in high esteem by these Jews, and now God comes down and talks to Joshua, and says, "Moses is dead." Moses is dead, Joshua.

As God is preparing you to enter into the land, he is go- ing to kick out all the human props, all the creature streams and reservoirs that we draw from. He is going to take them away. I'm sure that as Joshua wandered through the wil- derness, he relied heavily upon Moses. But "Moses is dead" now, God tells Joshua, "But I'm not." There are times in our lives when Elijah's brook has got to dry up so that we realize that Elijah's God never will. He'll kick out the props. It's a great point that when the man of God dies, the work of God goes on. The work of God will go on when the man of God dies. If the work doesn't go on, maybe it didn't need to go on. Maybe it was not a work of God. But when the man of God dies, God's work still goes on. There are a lot of times where we draw strength from other people, great Bible teachers that have been brought into our lives, and people that we look up to. But there is a danger in that. No matter how smart they are, no matter how eloquent they are, no matter how adept at teaching they are, they are creatures of the dust, whose breath is in their nostrils. We need to be brought to that point where we're looking to Jesus and to Him alone. We're not to draw our strength from oth- er people and those around us. We need to be brought to that point where it's God and God alone that we can go to and draw our strength from. There may be some thing or people in your life God is moving so you can see Him. We need to look to Jesus and Jesus alone.

In verse 2: "Moses my servant is dead; now therefore arise, go over this Jordan, thou, and all this people," It's an interesting word in there that a lot of people miss where the passage reads "this

Jordan." This Jordan. What is so particu- lar about this Jordan? Let's look at Joshua 3:15: "And as they that bare the ark were come unto Jordan, and the feet of the priests that bare the ark were dipped in the brim of the water, for Jordan overflowed all his banks all the time of harvest."

It was this Jordan at the flood season, when the Jordan was at flood stage. In the land of Palestine, there are two sea- sons, the dry season from May to October, and the rainy season from November to April. The harvest time usually falls around April, right at the end of the rainy season. Now the people in the land of Palestine are thinking, "All right, so what, there are a couple of million Jews camped over on the other side of the river. There is no way they're crossing this river. It's at the flood stage. It's raging. They don't have a boat. There is no bridge. There is no way they're crossing." But God April-fooled the Canaanites. They were in no way ready. Most commentators are not sure exactly where they crossed. But most will place it within a range. And inside that range, at flood season, there is no point where the Jordan River is less than two miles. So we're talking about a two-mile wide raging river at flood season. And yet God doesn't even bat an eye when He says this, He doesn't clear His throat, and He doesn't slow down. He says, "Moses my servant is dead; now therefore arise, go over this Jordan. I don't want you to wait until October when it dries up. Go cross this Jordan, right now."

I can imagine Joshua—"Thi. . .thi. . . this . . . this Jor- dan? I mean do you realize that it's flood season? It's a rag- ing river!" In preparation for entering into the land, God prepares you by calling you to do the impossible. What impossible thing has fear stopped you from doing? I want to encourage you to walk into the overflow; you can handle it. We can accomplish difficult things. But God calls you to do the impossible. And He doesn't even clear His throat, and doesn't hesitate when He says this. It's a principle you find throughout Scripture. Almost everything He calls us to do is impossible. Think about it. Jesus is walking on the water, and He tells Peter, "Step on out of the boat. Come on, take a walk with me."

I've tried it. It's impossible. You can't walk on water. It's impossibility. As Jesus is walking throughout the land of Palestine, He comes across a paralyzed man. I've dealt with some paralyzed people in the past. And He said, "Stretch forth your hand." Most paralyzed people that I know can't do that. It's impossibility. He asked this paralyzed person to stretch forth a withered hand. It's impossible. He called him to do the impossible. Jesus would go through and speak deaf ears would open and blinded eyes would see. These are impossibilities.

"Lazarus come forth." Lazarus is dead! He's in grave clothes and has been there for four days, and Jesus says "Lazarus come forth." God calls us to do the impossible. Not the difficult, but the impossible.

He also calls us to do other things that are impossible like "turn the other cheek." "Husbands love your wives as Christ loved the church." "Be ye holy as I am holy." They're just as impossible as "Lazarus come forth." They are for me, anyway. They are impossible things. I can't attain them.

In my first year as senior pastor, God said, "Build." I thought, "God, how could we with the little money in the bank we had, But we finished; because God said it, we did it. God prepares us to enter into the land by calling us to do the impossible: love your brother, forgive them that despite- fully use you. Again, impossibilities.

Verses 2 and 3 read, "Moses my servant is dead; now therefore arise, go over this Jordan, thou, and all this people, unto the land, which I do give to them, even to the children of Israel. Every place that the sole of your foot shall tread upon, that have I given unto you, as I said unto Moses." God says, "I am giving the land to you. It is a free gift. All you have got to do is cross over Jordan. You've got to tread upon it.

You've got to conquer the enemy. You've got to drive them out. There are a few things you've got to do, but I'm giving you the land. It's a free gift. Everything on which you tread, it's yours. It's yours; you can have it."

Sometimes we have difficulty drawing out what's Gods part, and what's man's part. We have the responsibility. He gave us the great commission: "Go ye into all the world." There is God's sovereignty, the giving of the land. And there is also the part where man has the responsibility to go in and cross the river Jordan. Tread upon it. Drive out the en- emy enter conquer occupy all those things that we must do. God gives, but we must take. Faith is not something that's passive. You can't just sit back in your rocking chair at home and say, "I have faith. God is just going to give me a victory. I'm going to sit back and trust God for it, and do nothing." It doesn't work that way. You will get nowhere in the land.

God said, "I give you the land as a free gift." But what if the children of Israel just sat on the other side of the Jordan and said, "He gave it to us as a free gift. I'm just going to sit right here and claim it. Hallelujah, it's mine. I don't need to cross Jordan. That land over there they are living in is mine." It doesn't make much sense. We laugh, but we do that in this Christian life from time to time, don't we? Man can cry to the earth, "Give me bread!" And the earth can cry back, "It's yours. It's a free gift. I will give you bread. But you'd better put in the plow. You'd better sow the seed. You'd better thrust in the sickle. You'd better grind the grain.

You'd better bake the bread. I give it to you. It's a free gift. But you've got to work for it." God says that He will free- ly give it, but we have got to work. Psalm 104:27-28 really draws this out in a good way: "These all wait for you, that you may give them their food in due season. What you give them they gather in."

You open your hands, they are filled with food. You give it, but they have got to gather. There is a side of faith that is not passive. Folks, faith is active. A lot of times when we use that word that is brought out in the book of Hebrews, rest, we get the idea of kicking back in the Lazy-Boy. But that's not what that word rest means and has to do with. There is a part of faith where you have got to resist the devil. You've got to study. You've got to work. You've got to drive out sin. You've got to resist and fight. Not in your strength, but in the strength that God gives you. Faith is not for the sluggard. It is not for the slothful. It requires activity.

Let's look at verse 7. "Only be thou strong and very cou- rageous, that thou mayest observe to do according to all the law, which Moses my servant commanded thee: turn not from it to the right hand or to the left, that thou mayest prosper whithersoever thou goest." We need to come to the point where we are willing to obey God no matter what. Often we'll look at verse 7 and 8 and say, "Okay, we need to read.

We need to study. We need to memorize." That's the way we sometimes interpret verses 7 and 8. But I think the key there is "only be thou strong and very courageous, that thou mayest observe to do according to all that I have written."

Obedience is the key. Obedience. It all hinges on obedience. If you study your Bible just to increase your knowledge, all that is going to do is make you proud; that's knowledge puffed up. But if you study your Bible with a heart attitude that I want to know this Bible, I want to know God, and know His word so that I may obey Him, then God will reveal Himself through His word. It's not that we need to study more. It's not that we need to memorize more. It's that we need to have the right heart attitude when we come to His word. We need to have that attitude that "I want to know God so that I may obey Him. No matter what He says, I may obey Him and do what He asks me to do." You may fall, but get back up and try again. Verse 7 tells Joshua to be strong and to be very courageous. And that's brought into the context of obedience.

It seems kind of odd that they are in there. "Be strong and very courageous to obey me." A lot of times we think of strong and courageous as Joshua heading into battle. We think of strong and courageous as people who are willing to lay down their lives for the Gospel. Strong and courageous is somebody who is willing to jump out in front of a bus to save a child. But God ties it into the context of strong and courageous enough to obey Him: "No matter what happens, no matter how many people look at you funny, no matter how many people make fun or pick at you, be strong and courageous and obey me."

The greatest endeavor in the Christian life is obedience. It's not doing great things, preaching great messages, all of those things. Obedience is the greatest exploit in the Chris- tian life. And it takes courage. And it takes strength. Obey no matter what. If the sky falls, obey God. If tomorrow finds you on the street, obey God.

A lifetime of knowing God through the Bible in order to obey Him is a foundational principle for entering into the land of Canaan. Walking in the overflow. I want to look at verse 5, because God gives a couple of revelations about Himself to Joshua as he's getting ready to go into the land. The first one He comes out with is in Verse 5: "There shall not any man be able to stand before thee all the days of thy life: as I was with Moses, so I will be with thee." I think we're all familiar with the verse "Jesus Christ the same yesterday today and forever." He is the same. He is immutable. Un-changing. He is perfect. And therefore being perfect, He cannot change. There is no need for change. He is perfect. He is unchanging.

Often we get in our heads the idea that all those exploits of the Christian life are for somebody else. They're for the Joshua's, they're for the Elijah's, and they're for the Paul's. "As I was with Moses, so shall I be with thee." Has God ever delivered a sinner? Yes. "As I have been with Moses, so shall I be with thee." Has God ever given anybody victory? "As I was, so shall I be." Has God ever revealed Himself in special ways to people? "As I was, so shall I be." It's not just for the great men of the past. It is for us to claim. I want to encour- age you to know wherever you are at in life, God is right there.

Chapter One: Walking in the Overflow

As he was with Moses, he shall be with you. Walk in your overflow.

Chapter 2:

Preparing for the Overflow

I will start chapter 2 with words from Joshua 1:10-18:

10Joshua then commanded the leaders of Israel, 11"Go through the camp and tell the people to get their pro- visions ready. In three days you will cross the Jordan River and take possession of the land the LORD your God has given you."

12Then Joshua called together the tribes of Reuben, Gad, and the half-tribe of Manasseh. He told them, 13"Remem- ber what Moses, the servant of the LORD, commanded you: 'the LORD your God is giving you rest and has given you this land.' 14Your wives, children, and cattle may remain here on the east side of the Jordan River, but your warriors, fully armed, must lead the other tribes across the Jordan to help them conquer their territory. Stay with them 15until the LORD gives rest to them as he has given rest to you, and until they, too, possess the land the LORD your God is giving them. Only then may you settle here on the east side of the Jordan River in the land that Moses, the servant of the LORD, gave you."

16They answered Joshua, "We will do whatever you com- mand us, and we will go wherever you send us. 17We will obey you just as we obeyed Moses. And may the LORD your God be with you as he was with Moses. 18Anyone who rebels against your word and does not obey your every command will be put to death. So be strong and courageous!"

When we really want something in life, we spend a lot of time and effort preparing for it. Athletes spend long hours training their bodies and honing their skills. Soldiers put themselves through training, readying themselves for combat. Years of schooling and preparation are demanded before one can aspire to be a doctor, a lawyer, an architect or an engineer. No matter how much interest, desire and natural inclination we possess, we still have to work hard and extend effort and dedication to reach our goal.

It is no different with the spiritual life. We cannot be- come spiritual, godly people until we get our priorities in order and are willing to invest time and effort pursuing spirituality. This presents a problem for Christians whose spiritual investments are diminished by the more immedi- ate demands of worldly pursuits. This is your day for walk- ing in the overflow, however there is a difference between cultivating the spiritual life and educating yourself to be- come, say, an engineer. Unlike engineering, the spiritual life cannot be captured solely by our own efforts and planning. We can work hard and become good engineers, but hard work alone will not make us spiritual people. So in the spiritual life we must allow God to be involved. It is true that we cannot become spiritual without engaging ourselves, but we cannot become spiritual either without God gracing, gifting and working on our behalf.

I remember trying to stay out of trouble; it used to seem trouble would always find me till the day I say yes to Jesus. If you don't know Jesus as your savior, invite Him in your life so you can walk in the overflow. The spiritual truths that I am talking about in the opening chapter of the book of Joshua help us prepare for this spiritual life that we are describing. The foundational principles set out in this chapter form the basic training that helps us enter the "land," which is our life in Christ. In the first chapter I see some highlights of tension between our own efforts and God's working. On the one hand, the land comes as a gift. It has certain enemies, but no enemy can stand before us, because God is with us. On the other hand, we saw that we have to engage in battle, too. We have to keep the Word of God central to our lives and worship, and we have to risk being strong and bold. In order to walk in the overflow, it is not always easy serving

God, but it can be done if you trust Him; He is able. As the darts are coming at you, keep the faith as I continue to explore these fundamentals with you. Yes, we are still in a basic training mode, still in spiritual boot camp.

We looked at God's words to Joshua. In these verses, Joshua gives instructions to all the people (verses 10- 11), and then he has a conversation with the two-and-a-half tribes that settled beyond the Jordan (verses 12-18). I feel it will help us enter the land, to walk in the overflow. Here is a truth I want to highlight: The purpose of entering into the land is to possess the land. "Then Joshua commanded the officers of the people, saying, 'Pass through the midst of the camp and command the people, saying, "Prepare provisions for yourselves, for within three days you are to cross this Jordan, to go in to possess the land which the Lord your God is giving you, to possess it"'" (vv 10-11). The word "possess" occurs four times in our text. In military affairs, the word "possess" means to gain control over a certain area by conquering and expelling its inhabitants. In Israel's history, the root of this word takes on a double force. In order to possess the land, the enemy must be dispossessed or driven out. Once that is accomplished, covenant life and responsibility can be engaged in the land. It may seem hard, but with God you are able. In the Old Testament, the words dispossessing and possessing were used in reference to physical enemies and physical land. But this always pointed to a deeper reality. For example, Psalm 16 declares: "The

LORD is the portion of my inheritance and my cup; Thou dost support my lot. The lines have fallen to me in pleasant places; indeed, my heritage is beautiful to me" (Ps 16:5-6). In the New Testament, we see that this inheritance, this pos- session, is identified with Jesus and all the blessings that are ours when we are in a relationship with him.

The apostle Peter says that believers have been "born again to a living hope through the resurrection of Jesus Christ from the dead, to obtain an inheritance which is imperishable and undefiled and will not fade away, reserved in heaven for you" (1 Peter 1:3-4). Paul says that believers have been "sealed in Him with the Holy Spirit of promise, who is given as a pledge of our inheritance, with a view to the redemption of God's own possession, to the praise of His glo- ry" (Eph 1:13- 14). God wants us to take possession of our lives in Christ, but in order to do this we must dispossess the enemies in our land, the enemies of the flesh, the world, and the devil. These foes cannot stand before us because we are in Christ, but we have to cross the Jordan and go to war with them.

As I walk in the overflow there has been a group of devils demons trying everything they can do to stop me from walking in the overflow, Do you have a closet in your home that is an utter mess and you have dreams of making it neat and useful? In order to possess that closet you must dispossess the mess! You have to begin by taking everything out of it, and then you have to throw away the junk, vacu- um the closet and wash down the walls. Then it is ready to be inhabited. Say you want to plant a field. First, you have to clear the land to make it ready for planting. You have to dispossess the things growing in the ground before you can sow the seed. So it is with our life in Christ. We want to be more loving people, but in order to possess this qual- ity of love, we must get rid of anger. We want to be more generous people, but in order to possess generosity, we must dispossess greed. We desire to serve in the commu- nity, but in order to possess this attribute of servanthood, we must dispossess selfishness. The whole time the enemy has attacked me, I have been able to walk in love. My friend and spiritual father says, "Go on down the way and wait." There were times I didn't understand, but thank God I went on down the way. You may be in a battle, you may be like me; my enemy is/was someone close to whom I call friend. This truth is extremely important, because it helps us to realize why we have to go to war. It gives us purpose as we face each new day. We are dispossessing the enemies of the flesh, the temptations of the world and the schemes of the devil, not as an end in themselves, not to earn our way into heaven, but to possess the life in Christ that is given to us by God. When we battle controlling bosses, deal with unreasonable parents, face overwhelming fears of rejection, or wage war against some deep sin in our life, the Lord calls us to battle in order to take possession of our life in Christ.

The battle is not about who will get a promotion, which marriage partner will prevail, finding a mate to relieve lone- liness, winning a lawsuit, impressing a church board, earn- ing God's approval, or having the perfect career. The battle is about trust, patience, self- control, integrity, honesty and godliness. It is all about facing our fears. Our goal is to pos- sess Christ and let Christ possess us. If we are not clear on our purpose, then we will get lost. Having a clear purpose is key in any war. So the question that arises is, what will it take to possess the land?

Our first thought might be of sharp minds and strong muscles, but not according to the Psalms. Here we receive the great insight that it is not by might or strength that we will possess the land, but by attending to our relationship with God. Listen to what the psalmist says about possess- ing the land: "Who is the man who fears the Lord? He will instruct him in the way he should choose. His soul will abide in prosperity, and his descendants will inherit the land" (Ps 25:12-13). Psalm 37 has four references regarding what it takes to possess the land: "For evildoers will be cut off, but those who wait for the Lord, they will inherit the land" (Ps 37:9). "But the humble will inherit the land, and will delight themselves in abundant prosperity" (Ps 37:11). Jesus formed the third beatitude from this verse. "For those blessed by Him will inherit the land; but those cursed by Him will be cut off " (Ps 37:22). "The righteous will inherit the land, and dwell in it forever" (Ps 37:29). The psalms say that we possess the land by fearing the Lord, waiting on him, being humble, receiving his blessings, and being righteous.

Here is another truth we learn from these verses: The result of possessing the land is to enter God's rest. The word "rest" appears in verses 13 and 15. Like the words "give" and "possess," "rest" is a covenant term, a word with deep theo- logical significance. Rest is described by God as "His rest." It is a place granted by God where there is peace and respite from enemies and the promise of the cessation of sorrow and toil in the future. Rest is a place where Yahweh will "plant" his people, where they will live without fear of being disturbed ever again. After six days of creation, God rested. He gave the Sabbath as a reminder to us to cease from our work and to wait on him. In all that I have been through and going through, I have rest. In Joshua, rest was associ- ated with entering the land and dispossessing enemies. The two-and-a-half tribes had entered into rest; now they were to help the other tribes enter into their rest. In the book of Judges, when enemies were subdued, the land would be said to be "at rest." In the New Testament, we discover that that rest is found in Christ. Jesus said, "Come to me, all who are weary and heavy-laden, and I will give you rest. Take my yoke upon you and learn from me, for I am gentle and hum- ble in heart, and you shall find rest for your souls. For My yoke is easy and my burden is light" (Matt 11:28-30). And here is what the writer of Hebrews says about this subject of rest: "For if Joshua had given them rest, He would not have spoken of another day after that. There remains therefore a Sabbath rest for the people of God. For the one who has entered His rest has himself also rested from his works, as God did from His" (Heb 4:8-10).

Isn't this what we are really seeking? We want a home where we are at peace, a secure place where we can feel content and whole. What we are doing is trying to recapture the Garden of Eden. We long for the new heavens and the new earth. But we can enter right now into the rest that is in Christ. He is the place where we stop striving for love and acceptance, stop running from fears and self-hatred and stop trying to satisfy the deep hungers of our souls. The interesting thing, however, is that we have rest not by escaping war, but by going into battle. We can't remain passive. We can't ignore the threats caused by heartache and addiction. We have to be honest, strong and courageous and willing to face these things. But then we cease from fighting, and we worship. We find rest in Christ, and we look forward to ultimate rest at his coming. This is your day.

I want to point something here that involves community: An essential element in possessing the land is for all Israel to fight together. Verse 2 emphasizes "all this people."

A very important exchange occurs between Joshua and the two-and-one-half tribes that settled east of the Jordan. Joshua reminds these people of the promise they made to Moses to help their brothers when they entered the land. When Israel defeated Sihon, the king of the Amorites, and Og, the king of Bashan, across the Jordan, Rueben, Gad, and the half-tribe of Manasseh wanted that land for their inheritance (Numbers 32). Moses was very angry with them for making this request, because he felt that granting this would discourage Israel from entering Canaan (just as when the twelve spies entered the land and ten of them reported the discouraging news that there were giants inhabiting that place). Moses did grant this land as an inheritance, but he made these two-and-one-half tribes promise to enter the land with Israel and fight with them. They would not return until the enemies were defeated.

What these tribes were asking for was second best. The lesson is clear: If we want to settle for second best, God will accommodate us. It was crucial that all Israel enter the land together. Community is a central theme in Joshua. Throughout this book, the community of Israel fights together and worships together. We will see that all Israel crosses the Jordan, all Israel is circumcised, all Israel celebrates the Passover, all Israel walks around Jericho, all Israel suffers when Aachan sins, all Israel reads Deuteronomy at Mt. Ebal and Mt. Gerizim. This points out the truth that all Israel is designed to experience life together in the land. Community is essential for possessing this life in Christ, and it is essential for going to war against the enemies in the land. But this important element to our warfare is often missing in our day and age. We were never intended to fight this war alone. It is to be waged by the people of God against the enemies of God. There is tremendous fear in being alone, but great encouragement in being together. This is why there is great value in being part of a community where there are real relationships and honest sharing, one in which there is healthy confrontation, supportive encouragement and a commitment to pray for each other. When part of the community is missing or is involved in sin, then the whole suffers. What happens to you affects me; my sin and my struggles affect you.

All too often, the problem we have in warfare is trying to go it alone. This is what Paul implies in Ephesians when he says that the whole body is growing into a mature man, "being fitted and held together by that which every joint supplies, according to the proper working of each individual part" (Eph 4:16). Here then are a few more truths that will help us prepare for war: The purpose for the war is to possess our life in Christ; the result of possessing the land is to enter into rest; an honest and healthy community of which we can be a part is essential to our life in Christ. It is work. God requires us to help our fellow brother; it's not about me, it's not about you, it is all about God. Let's walk in the overflow.

Chapter Two: Preparing for the Overflow

Chapter 3:

Positioning Yourself for the Overflow

Walking in the flow requires Loyal Leaders & Faithful Followers. Moses didn't want the job and flat out told God to "find somebody else."

Jeremiah thought he was too young. Jonah didn't like being a prophet to Nineveh and went to great lengths—and depths—to avoid being a leader. When Pastor Ruth died,

I was happy working as a youth pastor and I didn't think I was ready to pastor Calvary. And David was willing to wait on God to remove Saul before he took the place of leader- ship in Israel.

Reluctant leaders are often the best leaders. It's those who are power-hungry and eager to assert their authority that often does more harm than good. What I have ob- served is that there are more reluctant leaders in the church than there are those who are hungry for power and author- ity. In fact, some of you reading this may be thinking, "If he's going to start talking about leadership, then I may as well put the book down, because he's not talking to me. I'm certainly not a leader." You may be shepherds. You may be a Bible teacher. You may be a leader. Or you may have a position of leadership where you work. You may be a father or mother. Even if you aren't now, it is a likelihood that you will someday be in one of those positions. We are all lead- ers in one arena or another, whether CEOs of corporations or parents of small families. And we all need to know the biblical principles of leadership and authority.

Joshua offers us a model of Godly, biblical leadership.

As a Godly leader, you must be in touch with God, and this is the major difference between worldly leadership styles and godly leadership. Godly leadership requires a growing, developing, and daily relationship with God. The world only knows how to lead and manage from a worldly per- spective. The godly leader is able to see beyond the physical world of spreadsheets, statistics and management theories to the spiritual world that influences everything around us. God had made it clear to Joshua that to be successful Joshua had to stay in touch with his leader. Verses 7 & 8 emphasize that every leader needs to know God's word and obey God's will. The key is in understanding that even though you lead others, God is leading you. Just as others submit to your authority, you submit to His. This was the power of Jesus' leadership! After Jesus finished the Sermon on the Mount, the people were astonished because he taught as one who had authority. Yet about himself Jesus said, "…the son can do nothing by himself; he can do only what he sees his Father doing, because whatever the Father does the Son also does" (John 5:19).

It doesn't matter how large or small the leadership role may be, we cannot overlook our relationship with God.

Why is it so important that a leader stays in touch with God? It was said, "Whether a man likes it or not, if he's in a place of leadership he will be influencing others. He has no right just to consider himself. He must think in terms of his influence. This is part of the price of leadership! Not just the man himself, but what happens to those who follow in his footsteps is the serious responsibility of the leader. "This kind of responsibility demands that the leader stay in touch with his leader. As a leader you must take a tough stand. Look at Joshua 1:10-11. Because Joshua had been with God, he knew what the people needed to do, and he didn't hesitate to give the commands. Under Moses' lead- ership the people had delayed and hesitated about entering the Promised Land because of their fear and unbelief. What is stopping you from walking in the overflow? Joshua knew that for this generation it was now or never.

"But wait a minute, Joshua. Don't you need to think this over? Surely you're not going to make such a crucial decision so quickly?" Israel had spent 40 years preparing for this moment. There was no time to waste. It was now or never. Every leader must face the time when he must make a decision that will be unpopular. To be completely candid, being a leader isn't as glamorous as we may think. There are some painful aspects of leadership: criticism, weariness, loneliness, rejection and stress. Every normal, well-adjust- ed person wants to be liked, but a leader will not always be liked. And behind any worthwhile accomplishment there is a price to be paid. I learned that the hard way as we were building the church. It wasn't easy, but God was with us.

Any successful leader must be willing to make tough stands and pay the price.

I have learned as a leader you must be able to delegate responsibility. Joshua did this by working through his chain of command. Notice verse 10. You must also have a plan of action, and this is more than a slogan. As pastor, God have given me a vision to walk in the overflow. Joshua had a three-point plan of action. In v. 11 he commands the people to do three things: prepare, cross over, and possess. What was it that made Joshua successful as leader while Moses struggled in the same position? Does successful leadership require successful follower ship? Do the attitudes of the followers have an influence on the success or failure of their leader? I believe the reasons for Joshua's success as Israel's leader are seen in these verses from Joshua. Just as we need to examine our leadership skills, we also need to examine our follower-ship skills, too.

As you walk in the overflow, examine yourself. Look at verses 12-15. This bit of Israel's history is a testimony against selfishness. It's a statement of what it means to be the family of God. There's no room for selfishness in the kingdom of God. We are a family. Within the family those who are rich share with those who are poor. We're called to provide for the needs of the widows and orphans. Our responsibility to each other and to each other's needs is never fulfilled. As Paul put it, "Let no debt remain outstanding ex- cept the continuing debt to love one another." A characteristic of successful followers is their willingness to be united in a common task. Listen to how the people respond to Joshua in vs. 16-18. The unity of the church is the most powerful force against Satan's army. The disunity of the church is Satan's most precious ally. Every church that's torn apart by disunity and disorder, by pride and selfishness, Satan stands and laughs at their fruitless efforts. Every family where there is division between husband and wife, between par- ents and children, Satan dances with joy. But every church that stands united in love by the power of God's Spirit, who is made one by their selfless concern for each other's needs,

Satan is unable to stop them from marching on to victory. Every family where each member is respected and cher- ished, where love is freely given and freely received, Satan stands silent. Successful followers listen to their God-given leader's plan of action. They trust them because they know that they're in touch with God. Then they become united in the pursuit of a common goal. I have seen so many church- es and family suffer because of division put God first and walk in the overflow.

Chapter 4:

Trusting God in the Overflow

In the past three chapters I discuss Joshua 1 and 2, and we recognize God's promises of Victory and of His Presence with us. We see that as we obey, and as we meditate on God's Word, we come to experience the fulfillment of those promises. I see so much of the theme of trust in Joshua –past discovering that the basis of our trust is in the promise of God's presence and victory. That is what we rest on. That is why we let go and let God be in control. That is the source of our strength and courage. In this chapter as we continue to walk in the overflow, we have to let go and let God be in control. This does not mcan that we sit around and do nothing, but rather that we act on the prom- ises of God, that we live them out in fact I could go further and say that we only really experience the

Chapter Four: Trusting God in the Overflow

depth of God's promises in dangerous, uncomfortable, unsafe situations.

The more I have been under attack by a so-called preacher friend, the more I have seen God at work. It was and is a uncomfortable place to be but God gets the Glory.

You have to be able to rise even in evil, unsafe situations, as in Joshua 2. Living the Promises: I love what we see happening in this story. In the previous chapter, God has promised Joshua and the Israelites the land. He promised them victory "everywhere you set your foot" (1:3). And in this next chapter, Joshua gets busy. He secretly sends a couple of people to spy out the land, and especially the city of Jericho. My Bible doesn't say anything about God telling Joshua to send in the spies.

And if you remember back to Moses' time, he sent in some spies and it all didn't turn out to well. Didn't God just promise to give Joshua the whole land? Then why the need to send in the spies? Does that display a lack of trust on Joshua's part, a sort of taking matters into his own hands kind of thing? Why didn't he just trust God, rest on the promises, and march across the river and claim the land?

The questions become even more relevant if we sneak a peak ahead into chapters 5-6, where we have the story of the fall of Jericho. Remember how the city falls into the hands of the Israelites? They take the city simply by march- ing around it for seven days, and then God miraculously tears down the walls at the shout (yes, simply the shout) of the Israelite army. God had a plan for the fall of Jericho; He knew how it was going to happen. So why bother with this whole spy thing? They obviously weren't going to need de- tailed inspection on the military readiness of the people of Jericho. Why send the spies if God was going to do a mir- acle? Even worse, isn't this whole spy thing contrary to the very nature of what it means to trust God isn't it an example of Joshua acting in his strength rather than in God's?

To answer those questions, we need to know what the response of God was to Joshua's actions. Was Joshua rebuked? Punished for not believing? Chastised for not simply trusting? No, not at all. In fact, and this is fascinating, God says nothing in this chapter. He has lots to say in chapter 1, and more to say in chapter 3 and 4 and 5 and 6. In all those places, we read, "And the Lord said to Joshua"; but here it just says, "Joshua secretly sent two spies." Obvi- ously God was not upset at Joshua, or there definitely would have been consequences, as we will see in chapter 7. And in fact, there is a wonderful result to this spy story: meeting Rahab and having her become a celebrated woman of faith, seeing all her family saved. So clearly God blessed Joshua's actions, and God worked through Joshua's actions, even though God had a different plan for taking the city.

Chapter Four: Trusting God in the Overflow

Here is the lesson I see for myself. Sometimes it is okay for us to get busy and do the things that make the most sense. I believe that God gave us the ability to make decisions. We often take that and run with it and try to make all the decisions ourselves, without involving God in our daily lives, and that is wrong. But it is also wrong to never make decisions. That leads to disobedience: for example, if God tells us to go one direction, and we sit around waiting for Him to tell us whether to walk or run or take a bus, and end up staying in the same place, we have disobeyed God's call to go. Sometimes all He tells us is to go, and He leaves the method of travel up to us to decide.

He said, "Build." I heard the voice and we begin to walk in the overflow. Here is what I am trying to say: trusting God means both that we wait on Him for guidance and direction and leadership and it also means that we get going in the direction He points us in. Let me give you an exam- ple: whenever I sit down at my computer to write, I first read the Scripture passage again – even if I am just coming back from a 15 minute break. Then I pray. I ask God to speak to me, to show me what He wants to reveal to me and to us through His Word. Sometimes I sit there in prayer, waiting for all these great revelations to come flooding into my mind. But most of the time that doesn't happen! Most of the time, the ideas and revelations start to flow as I write. See the process? God speaks as I move, as I act. He often just brings it point by point. So you see that trusting in God means waiting for His direction, and then starting to head in that direction trusting Him for the power and abilities to get there. That is what I see here in Joshua 2. Even though God had a different plan for taking Jericho, Joshua was not wrong in sending in the spies. That wasn't an indication of a lack of trust or a lack of faith it was the right thing to do! God surprised them with a different ending, but God also honored Joshua for doing the smart thing by sending in the spies to get a handle on what was happening in Jericho at that time.

Sometimes in life we get stuck. We get in a rut, we feel like we're spinning our wheels; we're discouraged and down and going nowhere. Maybe that is how you feel about your life today, like you are kind of stuck. If so, think about this: are you stuck because you don't know where to go, or are you stuck because you do know where to go but are waiting for something else to happen before heading that direction? If you don't know where to go, then you need to pray and seek God for guidance, and wait and let go and listen. On the other hand, if you are stuck but you do know which way you should be headed, get going. This is your day make the necessary decisions. Stop waiting for each piece of the puzzle to fall into place before taking the first step and just get moving. God will lead. The Israelites had been stuck at this place before, 40 years earlier. They knew which way to go under Moses, but got scared and retreated. This time around, they still know which way to go and by the way, it is the same direction, but this time they get a little extra encouragement from the report of the spies: "The Lord has surely given the whole land into our hands; all the people are melting in fear because of us." (Vs. 24). That was the added bit of confidence that they needed. And maybe that is the added bit of encouragement that you need today. God has it under control.

If you are going in the direction He wants you to go in, trust Him to take care of the journey. You will find Him sufficient; you will find Him abundantly able to meet the needs along the road. That is the big message I want you to see: trusting God means waiting on Him for direction, and it also means using the minds and gifts that He has given us to head in that direction. As long as we head in that direction in His strength and not in our own, as long as we continue to trust Him along the way and even let Him make mid-course corrections, walking in the overflow, we can be confident that we are trusting Him and walking in His power and not our own.

There is another thing I learned in this passage: God goes ahead of us. Joshua does the smart thing and sends the spies in. They go to "the house of a prostitute," most likely because that was a place where foreigners wouldn't arouse a lot of suspicion and where they would be able to get a handle on what the people were thinking. What they find there is miraculous. Somehow word gets to the king and he sends in the henchmen. So much for "secret, undercover agents." But here is where the story gets interesting. Rahab the prostitute hides them, lies for them, sends the king's men off on a wild goose chase, protects them, gives them the information they need, and then provides their escape route. And in return, she and her family have their lives spared and Rahab takes a prominent place in the history of Israel and in Christianity because of her faith. Here is what this tells me: God goes ahead of us. And not only does He go ahead of us, preparing the way, preparing the hearts of people, revealing His fame and His glory, but He goes ahead of us and we find Him in strange and unexpected places.

These spies found God at work in a house of prostitution, in the faith of a prostitute.

I apply this to sharing our faith. We often look at the prospect of sharing our faith with some sinner like we are making a foray into enemy territory, crossing the lines into the "unknown," taking a big risk. We head into those situations feeling like it is our job to take God to people who don't know Him. There is this big, dark land, and we have the Light and we must take it into this dangerous place.

This spy story reminds us that God is already there ahead of us. We aren't going in carrying Him along with us, as if He wasn't there already.

On the contrary, we take opportunities to share our faith with the realization that the Holy Spirit is already there, already working, already prodding and pursuing. We are wisest and most effective when we recognize that God is there already and encourage what He is doing in people's lives. Sharing our faith isn't only about bringing people to salvation; that is the final step in the evangelism process.

There are lots of steps before that, lots of contacts and words and deeds and expressions of love, and lots of things that God is doing to reveal Himself and draw people to Himself. God is there ahead of us, and often we'll find Him in unexpected places. Be open to those places! Look for those opportunities to join God at work in establishing His Kingdom. And take the opportunities He provides.

As we walk in the overflow, God goes ahead of us and prepares the way. He has all sorts of things prepared for us, as Ephesians 2:10 reminds us: "For we are God's work- manship, created in Christ Jesus to do good works, which God prepared in advance for us to do." Where has God been calling you to go? What has He been telling you that you need to be obedient to? If you are feeling stuck, if you are uncertain about which direction to head or how to get started, then I want to first encourage you with the fact that God goes ahead of you. He has prepared the road and He knows where the journey is going to take you. And He knows what you need to get started. Walk in the overflow the promise of God is that He has prepared for us a great Kingdom, which He desires us to experience in this life as well as in the next. It is a Kingdom of joy, of freedom, and of power. God has invited us to experience this Kingdom through His Spirit. I encourage you to take some steps, to do the things that make sense in pursuing a more full expe- rience of God's Kingdom in your life, to walk in the over- flow so that you can also see God's Kingdom come to those around you. Walk In The Overflow.

Chapter Four: Trusting God in the Overflow

Section 2: Look What God Can Do!

Foreword by
Dr. G. Calvin McCutchen, Sr.

When I read the title of this book, "Look What God Can Do", it immediately caught my atten- tion. I am indeed proud to have the honor to offer some insight on what may have inspired the author to write this thoughtful and spirit- filled work.

The author had to overcome many obstacles and have had some strongholds to struggle with but he has stayed with the Lord and the Lord hasn't filed him. I had the honor of presiding at his election as Pastor of his first church, Cal- vary Baptist, Sapulpa, OK I preached the sermon for his In- stallation Service and since that time he has honored me by becoming an Associate of mine at Mt. Zion Baptist Church.

I am pleased that he looks upon me as a mentor and a close friend. I have carefully read the contents of this book. Look What God Can Do is more than an appropriate title for a book –

it is his testimony. The Lord has brought the author through many dangerous, toils and snare. He's not through with him yet. He is still growing in knowledge and wisdom of God. I am in agreement with Scott Gordon -- Only God can cause:

- The seasons to change

- The grass to grow

- The dew to form

- The geese to fly

- The dogs to bark

- The frog to leap

- The lightening to flash

Eyes to see, ears to hear, brains to think and hearts to beat.

Because we know that God can – let us worship Him – witness to Him – sing His praise – witness for Him – and obey His word. This book should challenge the reader to face life with Integrity and purpose. It should also lead us to a greater dependence upon God.

Dr. G. Calvin McCutchen, Sr. Pastor Mt. Zion Baptist Church ~ Tulsa, OK

Chapter 5:

Look What God Can Do

God has been good to me. When it seemed as though there was no way out, God sent His only Son, Jesus Christ to help me. The first scripture that came to

life was 2 Corinthians 5:17, which I will talk about later. The bible states in 2 Corinthian 4:7-10, 14: *"But we have this treasure in earthen vessels, that the excellency of the power may be of God, and not of us. We are troubled on every side, yet not distressed; we are perplexed, but not in despair; Persecuted, but not forsaken; cast down, but not destroyed."* Now looking at verses 14,17, and 18: Get this in your spirit. "Knowing that He which raised up the Lord Jesus shall raise us up also by Jesus, and shall present us with you. For our light

Chapter Five: Look What God Can Do

affiiction, which is but for a moment, worketh for us a far more exceeding and eternal weight of glory

While we look not at the things, which are seen, but at the things, which are not seen; for the things, which are seen, are temporal; but the things, which are not seen, are eternal. Amen. As I begin to tell how good God has been to me, I hope this will bless you where you are or help you to get to where you need to be. Look what God can do! Yes, look up and see what God can do. October 7, 1968, I was born in Sapulpa and lived with my grandparents until third grade. I moved with my aunt and her husband and their six children. There were also six other children living there for a total of 13 children. There were always many children there. When I look back, God has been good to me. I was always in the church house. School and church were a must as long as I lived at Route 2, Box 555; I was expected to attend school and church. I was in the choir, served as an usher, was a part of the youth group, youth leader, Sunday school, and served as youth president for the Canaan Dis- trict. That little, Old church still stands today! I thank God for my pastor at the time that was a role model and friend. As a child, life had many ups and downs, seemed like more downs than ups, but I persevered. I began to work at the age of 11 years old. I cut grass, cleaned houses, and made trips to the little store for family members and older ladies. At 12 years old, I worked for a man who lived up the street. About two years later, he was shot and killed. It is sad to say, but a blessing because he was a child molester and there is no telling how many children he may have molested. I know God has been good to me. I have had many bad times but God has brought me out. Now as I look back, I remember my 11th grade year, sitting at the dinner table at home playing a card game. That was another way I made money. My mother was in Tulsa visiting around the 15th of Novem- ber. The phone rang. It was the police in Colorado Springs, Colorado, calling to tell us that my oldest brother had been shot. Like any other brother, I was sad and began to think of all the good times we had, the fights and all the trouble we got into and the times he was there for me as a big brother. I rode with my mother, my two aunts and a cousin to Colorado. We drove all night and at about 4 a.m., the car had begun to act up in the middle of nowhere, so we pulled over (Little did I know, God was in control). Right up the street, a man had a shop behind his house. Fixed the car and we were able to make it to Colorado. After a twelve- hour drive, or longer, we found out that my oldest brother, whom I loved dearly, was dead. They pronounced him dead on the 16th of November 1986. Life had never been the same. I had to learn how to deal with the loss of my brother. I really needed somebody to talk to, but I didn't have any- body to help so I blocked everything and everybody out. I got so sick of people telling me they knew how I felt; no- body knew how I felt. I don't like to hear people say that to this day. I can write and tell story after story of all the bad things that I have been through. We have all had some bad times I just want you to see what God can do. After going through years of hell, I mean hell right here on earth – in and out of jail, shot, robbed, betrayed by so-called friends

I was on a one way street to hell. It seemed like I had no hope. I was sent to El Reno Correctional Center. My first hour there, after turning my self in to the police, I opened my bible to 2 Corinthians 5:17: *"Therefore if any man be in Christ, he is a new creature: old things are passed away; behold all things are become new."* It was as if God had actually spoken to me for the first time! I had never heard God speak. I began to weep and read on and the Word became life to me. God began to deal with me; I had been running and just could not run any more. Each day for nine month, I read and studied God's Word. It became life to me. I should have been dead but the grace of God had saved me sinner. Yes, I understood God loves me and that has changed my life. God brought me out of all the hell I was in. After taking him as my Lord and the free Gift he gave me, His only Son, I can say I am more than conqueror. (Can I tell you that you can be an over comer) When I took Jesus as my Savior, I came to know that a blessing was just around the corner and when you see that, you can look into the mirror of life and see deliverance right around the corner. I also found love. Look what God can do. When life had me down, God showed me love. In the scripture, this exactly where I saw the great Apostle Paul as he was writing to the church of Corinth just 25 years after the death of our Lord and Savior Jesus Christ. You see, Paul's entire ministry was a graphic, invaluable and continuing illustration of God's love. Paul knew about weakness. I was weak and needed some help and began to read the letters of Paul. Paul knew about the calamities of life. Even as a Christian and in the midst of suffering, God showed me love in these last nine years of my life. I thank God for the love that I have re- ceived from the Lord Jesus Christ. It takes love to be a Christian in this world today. Paul knew something about love and there is still much I have to learn from this passage of scripture. It has been helpful for me and I believe this book will be helpful for anybody who reads, "Look what God can do". In the book of 2 Corinthians 4-8, when I see where I am today it must be God. Can I tell you if it had not been for the Lord on my side, and the love that he has given me; I don't know where I would be. Paul said in verse 7, "But we have this treasure in earthen vessels (in other words, we have this treasure lodged in a weak body), that the Excellency of the power may be of God, and not of us." I had to take God at his Word. Paul is saying that this thing, this source of strength, this source of love and courage is all prevailing power. This exceeding greatness, this thing I cannot explain, must be from God. He took me, a sinner, who was lost and had no way out and helped me in a time of trouble. He keeps getting me through rough times. It seems like every time I have a need for something, God supplies it. He keeps holding me up. When I wanted to give up. God sends help. He is always on time. This thing called God's love keeps me going. As Pastor of Calvary Baptist Church, God has been the leader and has shown up and is doing a great work. God has been good to me and it must be from God. I could not have made it by myself. It can't be from me. I would have given up a long time ago. God's power keeps making a way for me when I don't deserve it. God's strength keeps pushing forward when the world is pushing me back. God's authority keeps me agile when my enemies are trying to knock me off course. It can't be me. It can't be something I did. Lots of people say I would not make it, but God has been good. Some are stilling trying to pull me down, but God said, "No weapon that is form against me shall prosper". God is good. If I were preaching this, I would tell you to tell somebody – it must be God. It had to be God. Let me tell you this, I know it was God. I know it was God who save my life, I know it was God who made me right I know it was God who brought me out of those walls I know it was God who got me out I know it was God who called me I know it was God who taught me when my back was against the wall it was God. When my luck had run out it was God. When I was on my way out God said, I'll be your strong tower, I'll be your living water You see, I was like the woman at the well, full of sin and in need of a drink of living water. God showed up! "Look what God can do" He is the God of my salvation and will be the God of your salvation. When I was called to pastor, my pastor, Dr. McCutchen told me, "Do the best you can and God will do the rest." Since then, I have been doing my best and watching God do the rest. He has been am "Am: or should I say, "The Great I Am." I can look up and say look what God has done. All things are made possible through Him. This is why I give Him praise every day. I tried everything but one day, I tried Jesus and I have never been the same. It had to be God. Paul knew that it had to be God. Paul knew that through all the beatings, through all the persecution, through all of his affiictions, the shipwreck, his travels, his imprisonment and the turbulence of life, the love demon- strated in life was driven by his relationship with God. In fact, if you turn just a few pages with me in 2 Corinthians to Chapter 11, verse 24, you will see where Paul simultaneous- ly gives you an autobiography of his suffering...love and courage. You may be able to relate to some of this in your own life. Verse 24 says: *"Of the Jews five times received I forty stripes save one". (I got whipped 39 times) but I pressed on.* Verse 25 says: *"Three times I was beaten with rods, once I was stoned, three more times I suffered shipwreck, a night and a day I spent in the deep;" But I pressed on.* Verse 26 says: *"In my journeys, saw the perils of water, the perils of robbers, the perils of my own country men, the perils of the heathen, the perils of*

Chapter Five: *Look What God Can Do*

the city, the perils of the wilderness, the perils of the sea, and the perils of being around false brethren; Verse 27: *"I was weary and in pain, I was hungry and thirsty, I was cold and naked."* But I pressed on. Someone once said that courage is not the absence of fear but the willingness to push on in the face of it. Paul went through some stuff and he knew it could not have bee him; it had to be God who was getting him through. That is why I know that if you can relate to some of what Paul went through, the next few verses will be a word for you: Knock down, but never knock out. Paul said it must be God. How do I know that? Well look at verse 8 in 2 Corinthians. I don't know who is read- ing this but somebody needs to personalize this today. If you are that person, I want to replace the word "we are" with the words "I am".

"We are troubled on every side, yet not distressed. "I am troubled on every side, but I am not distressed. The word distresses come from the Greek meaning to have no way out. Another way of looking at it is like this: God is telling you that you may be hard pressed, but you are not crushed. You may have troubles all around you (I've been there), you may be hedged in from every corner, but you are not hemmed in. You may be persecuted, but not forsaken. You may be pursued, but never abandoned. You may have prob- lems, but don't stop. You may be hurting, but you are never abandoned. You may be cast down, but never cast out. In fact, one translation of the scripture describes God's word as to say

I've been knocked down but not knocked out. How many people how it feels to be knocked down? Knocked down on your job? I worked for a tree company that tried to keep me down every way they could. Knocked down in your health? My wife got sick right after she had our daughter, but God said that by His stripes, she was healed. Knocked down on your finances? Have you been broke and didn't know which way to go and God showed up? Knocked down in your life? Knocked down in your life? Knocked down by lies: Knocked down by words? Or, have you ever just been plain knocked down like a boxer that had gone 15 rounds in a heavyweight bout? That boxer, in the course of that fight, had taken some shots. I have had to take many shots and I am still taking them as I write this book. But, God is still good.

Just like the old boxer in the ring you will feel the pain of those body blows you will take some shots to the jaw you will take your scars you will take your wounds in the ring. And, sometimes during this life in the ring, you will un- doubtedly go down. When you go down, you will be face to face with the mat. You will get face to face with defeat. It is you against your opponent and your face is lying against the mat. Just like that boxer that has been hit with a tough blow, you are trying to get it together because when you took that hit, you were a little disoriented for a while. When you got hit, you felt the pain for a while. When you got hit, you felt like you wanted to just stay down. You were

Chapter Five: Look What God Can Do

struck down and you were knocked down. But, just when you thought it was over, just as the walls of the pain started closing in on you, just when that clock started ticking on you, just as they started to count you out – Jesus stepped in. When Jesus stepped in (praise God), you can look up to heaven unto the hills which cometh our help and receive your courage. When you received your courage, you said, I can look up to that mountains! I can beat that giant! I am going to make it to my knees and pray. I am going to get on my feet and walk. I am going to stand up and give him praise. I am go- ing to lift my eyes unto the Lord… and look what God can do. When life is trying to strike me down, when the devil has tried to knock me down, I can say in Jesus' name, I will not be knocked out. I will not be struck down. I will not be cast out. I looked unto heaven and I saw His mercy on my life. I saw His blessing, I saw His goodness. People have been trying to take me down, but I saw His power. People were trying to get me to fight, but I saw His peace. People were trying to take me away from myself, but I saw His provision. The invisible became visible. The untouchable became touchable. I can hear the unheard of. I can look up and say look what God can do. God is right around the corner. If you know Him, you ought to put this book down and call and tell somebody about the goodness of God. Call a sinner friend; it is all about God, It is God! It's incredible and yes seemingly impossible to think about where you have come from and what you have come from and not give Him praise…Amen? If you think about what He has done and brought you through and NOT want to shout, then just tell Him how much He means to you. Put this book down and give Him some praise. It will be all right, even if you are with somebody, God still desire the praise. It's all about God. You are where you are because of Jesus Christ. Even when we don't so right God has shown His love. It's all about God. When life seems like it is not going your way, it's all about God. When the world is not treating you right, when you feel knocked down, it's all about God. Beloved re- joice when glory is revealed, I want to end this chapter with 1 Peter 4:12-13: *"Beloved, think it not strange concerning the fiery trial which is to try you, as though some strange thing happened unto you: But rejoice, inasmuch as ye are partakers of Christ's suffering; that, when his glory shall be revealed, ye may be glad with exceeding joy."* When the glory is revealed. Look closely to what is being said to you: Beloved rejoice when the Glory is revealed. Beloved, rejoice when the glory is revealed. When you are hurt, when you've been afflicted with pain, Beloved, rejoice when the glory is revealed. When you've been burdened down with stress and worry. Beloved, rejoice when the glory has been revealed. You've been hard pressed, hemmed in and forsaken. You've been knocked down, struck down and kicked around. If you've been around the block and back again on the streets of hard knocks, God will whisper in your ear: Beloved, I am speak- ing to you. Beloved, I need to hear from you. Beloved, you are not the things you think you are. Beloved, I know what you are dealing with. I know about the fiery trail that is trying to take you out. I know about the hurt that is vexing your spirit. Beloved, I am not going to let you fall. I am not going to let them harm you. Beloved, rejoice. For when the glory has been revealed; when you have gone through the fire of affiiction; when iron has sharpened iron; next time, cry to me. I am going to open up the windows of heaven. I am going to lift you up to higher. When you are troubled, I'll lift you up. When you are cast down, I'll lift you up.

When you need courage, I'll lift you Up. You've been per- secuted, but not forsaken. You've been cast down, but not destroyed. You've been knocked down, but never knocked out. You've been put down, but never put out. You've been held down, but never held out because He's marvelous. He's marvelous. He's marvelous in the noonday. He's marvelous in the morning time He's marvelous in the midnight hour. He's marvelous for how He saved me.

He's marvelous for how He made me. He's marvelous. for what He does. He's marvelous for how He loves. He's marvelous because whatever is going on in our lives, what- ever we know we can't handle on our own, God will remind us through His word and through His people that we can look up when life has got us down, In fact, I want to say in this walk of life, another sermon that has helped me the most is the one that Dr. G. Calvin McCutchen wrote and preached: "When God Does Not Divide The Water." This has helped me to see that God has water-dividing power.

In 2 Corinthians 4:17, you will see how God describes what we define often times as crisis in our life and really how

we should look at obstacles that come our way in the jour- ney we call life. Let's look first in verse 14 where He said: "Knowing that he which raised up the Lord Jesus shall raise us up also by Jesus, and shall present us with you. In verse 17 he said. "For our light affliction, which is but for a moment, worketh for us far more exceeding and eternal weight of glory," (18th verse) "While we look not at the things which are seen, but at the things which are not seen: for the things which are seem are temporal; but the things which are not seem are eternal." What we weigh ourselves down with,

God will call a light affiiction. That issues at your job a light affiiction. That problem with your friend a light affiiction. The attack that you are dealing with a light affiiction. For God says that He is working a far exceeding and eternal weight of glory. God said seek the things that are eternal.

Seek the things that are not seen. Lay up your treasures in heaven. Be courageous. I promise you, God is right around the corner for you today. Remember, success is never final failure is never

Chapter Five: Look What God Can Do

fatal but with God on your side it will be courage that will count. This is only to help somebody know that God is able. Look what God can do.

Chapter 6:

Rags to Redemption

Psalms 107:1-9 " O give thanks unto the LORD, for he is good: for his mercy endureth for ever. Let the re- deemed of the LORD say so, whom he hath redeemed

from the hand of the enemy; And gathered them out of the lands, from the east, and from the west, from the north, and from the south. They wandered in the wilderness in a solitary way; they found no city to dwell in. Hungry and thirsty, their soul fainted in them. Then they cried unto the LORD in their trouble, and he delivered them out of their distresses. And he led them forth by the right way, that they might go to a city of habitation. Oh that men would praise the LORD for his goodness, and for his wonderful works to the children of men! For he satisfieth the longing soul, and filleth the hungry soul with goodness."

Look at another verse of God's word on what God can do. How do you go from rags to redemption? The question came to me: what is your next step? Looking for the answer, I began to explore the scriptures. The Lord had given me much to write about. Walk with me with your mind cen- tered on God and as you have your mind set on God, I want you to think about some things in your life. When you finish this book, I pray that it will help you see what God can do to help you stand strong in this Christian race and prepare for the weeks ahead. The spirit told me that it is time for someone to focus on this. When I gave my life to Christ, I had to take the next step in this chapter. I want you to think about your next step. You may be getting out of prison or in a jail cell. What is your next step with God?

What is your next step in your job? What is your next step in your life? What is your next step in your career or your business or ministry? What is your next step? You see, if we are ever going to go from a situation that is nothing but ragged, nothing but worn out, nothing but tattered, scared and wounded, then we are one day going to have to identify, confront and then act upon our next step. When I was in El Reno, I had to face up to, and then act on what God was doing. I had to take the next step. When you look at this scripture, you can see that God is clearly demonstrating to you in His word that there are benefits attached to taking the next step. He was telling me to move from a mainte- nance mentality, to move from an attitude of procrastina- tion, to move away from a spirit of slothfulness and slug- gishness regarding positive change in my life to have earthly as well as eternal benefits. In other words, God was telling me that with Him on my side, whatever the situation might be, I can move from rags of my situation to the redemption of God. When I opened my bible and read in Psalms 107 that God said: *"Give thanks to the Lord, for he is good: for his mercy endureth for ever."* I'm only writing on look what the Lord can do. "Let the redeemed of the LORD say so. " To be redeemed means to be delivered, to be set free or released.

If you are reading this book, I hope you are redeemed of the Lord. You, as a person of God, know you shouldn't ever be here today? I must say, I should have been dead sleeping in my grave. I thank God for saving a sinner like me. When I look back over my life and know I was doing wrong, when I knew I was moving in the wrong direction, look what the Lord can do. Let the redeemed say so. I knew that I wasn't doing right by God and I don't have a problem saying so.

Now I have a testimony. Now I am a witness. Now I know something I didn't know then.

Chapter Six: Rags to Redemption

Psalms 102:2 says *"Let the redeemed of the Lord say so, whom he hath redeemed from the hand of the enemy."* All the redeemed of the Lord have this in common: somewhere along the line, somewhere in our lives, somewhere in that crooked road of life, we suf- fered. We fought for something. We have been through some things and through all the suffering, the battles, the hurts, the wounds, the scars, the problems, the valleys and the mountains, the infirmities, the lies and attacks, we have seen the salvation of God and we now have reason to praise Him. We have reasons to praise Him or should I say I have a reason to praise Him. I have reason to give Him glory. I have reason to give Him the honor because when I was hungry with nothing to eat. I know I couldn't have made it on my own. When I was on the verge of homelessness, I couldn't have done it without him. I remember sleeping a few nights in a parked car with nowhere to go, no money in my pocket. When I was dealing with physical affiictions, I saw God show up." Look what God can do." When the diabetes, the arthritis, the cancer, the high blood pressure was attacking the personal health in my family, I am able to say in the name of Jesus and watch it go. There is power in that name. He made a way out of no way. He came in right on time. He supernaturally changed the natural. Just like the children of Israel, just like he told Moses. He told us fear not, be still and see the salvation of the Lord your God.

When God did his work, I had to start doing my work. When God took a step toward me, I took a step toward him. When God spoke to me, I started praying back to him. As the prayers went up, the blessing started coming down. As the prayers kept going up, my faith started growing because the bible says that your faith will come by hearing and hearing by the word of God. As my faith grew I began to realize that no weapon formed against me shall prosper and that every tongue that shall rise against thee (in judgment) shall be condemned. The enemy will be cast away in Jesus name. Lack will be cast away in Jesus name. Worry shall be cast away in Jesus name. Every burden shall be lifted off in Jesus name. Demons tremble at the sound of His name. It was time to take my next step out of bondage. It was time to take my next step out of prison. It was time to take my step out of the streets. It was time to take my next step out of that bad relationship. I thank God I have the best wife a man can ever have and that I trust God that He'll have mercy on me, that He'll protect me, that He has taken me from rags to redemption; and that all things will come together for the good of them that love the Lord. He is worthy to be praised, understand that you should know His goodness. Many of us have seen things and heard of things that can only be explained by the presence of God. When a bullet with my name on it was shot at me near point blank range, somehow I survived. All I received was a scare. "Look what

God can do." When I received approval for something that I knew I had no business getting approved for; my money was funny and my change was strange; my situation was suffering; my bills was multiplying; and I knew it wasn't supposed to go that way. Somehow, God made a way for me. I have seen His great works. I have experienced His mercy upon me, and as the redeemed of the Lord I know that He has rescued me from the hands of the enemy and I give Him thanks. One thing I learned is

God will tell you when you need to take your next step. The reality of this is that God has rescued me from some very hostile clutches. Look at Psalms 107:3; this may be a word for you. If you want to know more about God and what God has for your life, I ask you to look at these scriptures with me and think about where you are in regards to your next step and where you want to go in life. In regards to the ragged situation that you are currently trying to understand and deal with and the redemption that waits for you as you take a step toward God; in relation to the position that is rightfully yours on earth and in heaven and what God will give you to fulfill His will for you in your life, look at this closely and personalize it for a moment. Think about that situation of yours that you are just simply tired of dealing with and you need a change in it right now. Close your mind to everything but that thing you need to change; that thing you need to take the next step. It is important to think on these things because God wants you to know that not only does He knows those whom He has redeemed, but He also knows what you have done to stay where you currently are. God will tell you when you need to take your next step. The bible says that God gathered His redeemed saints from out of the lands, from the east, and from the west, from the north and from the south. Whether you are in Tulsa, Sand Springs or Sapulpa, Oklahoma; or Texas, God can gather and change you. God will push and pull you toward him when He is speaking to you. He will nudge and whisper to you when He wants you to come to him, He will urge and encourage you when He wants you to take the next step in your life. Psalm 104:4 says, *they wandered in the wilderness in a solitary way; they found no city to dwell in."* God said He saw you wandering in a solitary way (He saw you when you felt like you were all alone and didn't believe He existed in your life). As you wandered aimlessly in your journey, as you roved through the wilderness, as you sought the things of the world, as you looked at the next woman and looked at the next man, as you wandered in these places, I saw you when you found no city to dwell in. I know that did not fill the void that is in your life; that didn't heal the wounds of your losses; that didn't remove the scars and pain of the past; that did not come to any conclusions from your jour- ney. Now you are here. The bible says in Psalm 107:5, *Hun- gry and thirsty their soul fainted in them".* The

American Bible translation says: *"Hungry and thirsty their life was wasting away within them."* You died because of one thing that you used to do that you don't do any more. You died when you stopped dreaming. When you stopped dreaming, you stopped believing in your own personal vision for your life. You stopped giving and trusting in God for the provi- sion. You stopped directing and navigating and began weaving and wandering. You stopped pushing yourself to the top and were pulled to the bottom. You stopped speak- ing positives in your life and the lives of the people around us and started believing on the negatives. We stopped taking the next step. We settled for the rags of life and stopped pursuing the redemption. The bible says who shall separate us from the love of God that Jesus Christ came to give us life and life more abundantly. He is our present help in our time of trouble. And when they cried to the Lord in their trouble, my God shall supply all the need. The bible says that He will deliver you out of your distresses; that He will lead you toward the right way; that He will give you city of habitation; that he will satisfy your longing soul.

He'll make what is weak, strong. He'll turn your problems into promises. He'll turn your turmoil into triumph, your valleys into victories. Psalm 23:4 says, "Yea, though I walk through the valley of the shadow of death, I will fear no evil: for thou art with me; thy rod and thy staff comfort me." This is what helped with my brother's death.

When I under- stood those verses. Psalm 23:5-6; *"Thou preparest a table before me in the presence of mine enemies..."* You anoint my head with oil; my cup runneth over. Surely...Surely...Surely goodness and mercy shall follow me all the days of my life. When I got saved, I had to get rid of some old friends. God next steps will remove your old garments and put on your new garments.

It's time to lose the rags. I'm ready for redemption. I was ready to take the step. Well, I have just one more step I want you to take with me. I want you to come with me to the book of Mark, chapter 10, verses 46-51: *"And they came to Jericho: and as he went out of Jericho with his disciples and a great number of people, blind Bar-ti-mae-'us, the son of Ti-mae'-us, sat by the highway side begging. And when he heard that it was Jesus of Nazareth, he began to cry out, and say, Jesus, thou Son of David, have mercy on me. And many charged him that he should hold his peace: but he cried the more a great deal, Thou son of David, have mercy on me. And Jesus stood still, and commanded him to be called. And they called on the blind man, saying unto him, be of good comfort, rise; he calleth thee. And he, (Bartimaeus) casting away his garment, rose, and came to Jesus. And Jesus an- swered and said unto him, 'what wilt thou that I should do unto thee?' (What do you want from me?) The blind man said unto him, Lord, that I might receive my sight. And Jesus said unto him, 'Go thy way; thy faith hath made thee whole.' And immediately he received his sight, and followed*

Jesus in the way." Battimaeus was a man that was honest with him- self about a couple things. You may want to underline these thoughts and principles and refer to it as you enter into your next step. Bartimaeus recognized at least these three things:

1. He recognized that he did not like his current situa- tion and desired change.

2. He understood that the change that he so badly de- sired would take action.

3. He knew that he could not see the change without the help of God.

He had lost his physical sight, but knew that if he could just come to Jesus, that he would receive his sight, that he would be healed. This is the principle or thought I want you to receive; you may not be physically blind, but because you haven't taken your next step with God, you still can't see.

You may not like your current situation, but because you haven't taken a step forward with the Lord by your side, nothing has changed. You may want your change to occur so badly you can taste it, but if you haven't taken any action toward it, you are standing still. Bartimaeus recognized that he did not like his current situation. He was ready to take action, and most importantly, he knew that the change he really wanted could not receive on his own. He understood that he needed to reach and speak to God. But there was something he did which often times when reading this very familiar scripture we miss: look at verse 50. The bible says that as he was called by Jesus, "and casting away his gar- ment, rose, and came to Jesus. This is the point I want to make to you: if you want to take your next step, you have to cast away your old garments and come to Jesus. "Look what God can do." I had to get rid of some things that were hold- ing me back. You have got to put on a new garment. You've got to take off those old rags of bitterness. Take off those old rags of anger and that means putting on a new smile…. a new attitude a new mind a new heart. The Bible says be- cause He is the God of covenant He is the most-high God He is the Eternal God He is an all-powerful God. When I fall, He lifts me up. When I fail, He forgives me. When I'm afraid, He is my courage. When I'm hungry, He feeds me.

When I'm lost, He finds me. Thank you, Jesus, Jesus the heart-fixer Jesus the mind-regulator. Jesus the bond-break- er Jesus the Alpha and Omega. Jesus the living water Jesus who gives seed to the sower Jesus who gives bread to the hungry Jesus who breaks the mountains Jesus who fills the valley Jesus who crushes the devil Jesus who was wounded for our transgression; bruised for our iniquities. The chas- tisement of our peace was upon Him, but with His stripes we are healed. The only one that can help you as you take your first step from rags of this world to the redemption of God. Are you ready to receive peace? Are you ready to receive the joy that you desire and deserve? not empty joy, but complete, unconditional,uncompromising joy. The bible says in James 1:17, *"Every good gift and perfect gift is from above…"* Times may be tough and things may hurt right now, but even though you may have fallen, God say you can get back up and get back in line. I heard the songwriter say, "We fall down… but we get back up… A saint is just a sinner who fell down." Just remember, Jesus said that I have come to give you life and life more abundantly. If you believe in His word, the bible said that it would not come back void. Your joy is right around the corner. I pray that you have done an examination and that you desire to learn more about God and what God has done for your life. Take the next step of your life. Don't be afraid. Don't wait. Don't delay. "Look what the Lord can do." What is your next step? What are you going to do differently today and tomorrow then what was done yesterday? When are you going to try it God's way? God is waiting to show you His glorious plan and it's right around the corner. Come to him. God Bless you. "Look what God can do."

Chapter 7:

Press On

I want to help someone to press on. May these words of God comfort and challenge you to look what the Lord can do while pressing on. Philippians 3:12-14 says. "Not

that I have already obtained this or have already reached the goal; but I press on to make it my own, because Christ Jesus had made me his own. Beloved, I do not consider that I have made it my own; but this one thing I do; forgetting what lies behind, I press on toward the goal for the prize of the heavenly call of God in Christ Jesus." The greatest thing that can happen to us as Christian is that we become heav- enly-minded. I describe heavenly-minded as to live every part of your life with the goal of entering tin heaven having completed the purpose for which God has called you. To be heaven-minded is not to wait for heaven when we die, but to push toward the goal of entering heaven having finished what God has called you to accomplish. This passage reveals three important principles to me when we have yet attained what we are called to take hold of. We have not reached perfection, and we are to press on toward the call. Those principles are: We have not yet attained, or literally, have not laid hold of the purpose of our calling. I took the next step and saw what the Lord could do and was doing in my life from El Reno to Calvary. When I entered into fellowship with Christ by surrendering my life to Him it did not mean I automatically accomplished everything that Christ would have me to do as a new Christian. I had not yet laid hold of my calling. Even as an older Christian, you may not have found the purpose in which you were called. Jesus is the door that we must enter in order to begin our new life and begin our journey toward Heaven, but entering that door is not the finish line. It is a major error to think once we have become a Christian and gotten our ticket to heaven we have reached our goal.

We have not reached perfection. Even thought we may go to church, sing and pray, we are not there yet. We have not reached maturity and before your spiritual life can take root; your flesh nature must be crucified. When we become born again into the kingdom of God, we are set free from the bondage of sin and are no longer driven by the flesh. It is our responsibility to bring our hearts and minds under subjection to Christ. Each time I look back on my life, I am amazed at how far God has brought me. I should stand determined to never return to where I have been. Therefore, my focus in not on my past, but on my goal of winning the race God has set before me.

We are to press on toward the call. When I think I have arrived, and I am as far as I can go, God works in my life and I began to grow more. If I look back and think I have hit the mark, I will stop growing and eventually start sliding, but in Christ I am encouraged by my past and given the strength to reach ahead toward my calling. I can only overcome this life by His strength. Only He has the power to give me endurance to keep reaching ahead but I press on, that I may lay hold of that for which Christ Jesus has also laid hold of me. My earthly goal is to press on so that I can take claim to the calling that God has for my life. I am to strive to find the purpose for which God transformed my life and equipped me to achieve. God did not change your life just so you can live anyway you desire. God called you for a purpose. To find that path of life, you must be found faithful. Each step requires faithfulness to find the next step. As we press toward Christ-likeness, we should examine our live and identify those things that tempt or lead us to temp- tation. Sadly, most people cast off the eternal and cling to what will definitely pass away. If I were earthly-minded, I would value worldly things because I wouldn't believe God's promises. So how do we get eternally minded and focus toward the calling of God? This passage reveals two critical areas that help give us that heavenly perspective. First, we must determine what is of real value so that we can count all other things as nothing in light of the excellence of the knowledge of Christ. In Matthew 13:44, Jesus tells of a man who wanted to purchase a field. When he inspected it and found out that there was a treasure buried in it, he took all of his money out of the bank to buy the field. The crowd said that field is not worth it, but he knew the real value.

Once we find the real value of things, all other things are worthless. I heard a choir sing a song, "Lord you are more precious than silver and more costly than gold." Paul says, "I count all things as rubbish…" it is important to recognize that what the world presents as treasure is in fact waste without comparing it to what is valuable. The purpose of acknowledging this spiritual reality of these things is so that

we can let go and leave what is behind and press ahead for what God has laid before us. Look what the Lord has done. My passion should be to find God's calling and achieve what God has set me apart to fulfill. The only way I can live this Christian life and fulfill God's purpose is to reach ahead. When I lay hold of what God has revealed, I contin- ue to press on to the next step. Your purpose is not fulfilled in one act of obedience, but in a lifestyle of continuously reaching for God's purpose. As long as Jesus Christ is my goal, I can press ahead against obstacles and anything that demands my attention or attempts to draw me away. The task as pastor of one of God's greatest churches for the last several years and looking to Jesus who has kept me in my right mind and helped me to see what the Lord can do and have done and to press on is to live in complete obedience with a heaven-minded focus. I can't reach ahead if I am looking back to see what I am missing. If my heart is back in the world, I will not have the passion to press ahead. If my heart is on what I am leaving behind, I will eventually become discouraged and quit. If you look back, it is because you value what is behind. Hebrews 5:1 says, "Therefore, leaving the elementary teaching about the Christ, let us press on to maturity." This is Paul's life goal and this is his goal for us. He is writing and working for this goal. Let us press on to maturity. Let's leave the elementary teaching about Christ and press on to maturity. Don't lay foundations again.

Leaving the "elementary teaching about Christ" means we should not occupy ourselves so much with Christian issues that can't be resolved. A lot of scripture is a mystery to some, and others would rather argue about issues of scrip- ture and neglect the glory of the gospel and how to use it to grow into maturity and holiness. In other words, instead of arguing about theological and denominational stuff, prac- tice how to grow with them. The need is not to argue on bible issues, but to stand on them and live by then. The problem is not bible knowledge, but lack of fruitfulness in life. Let us press on to maturity! Nevertheless, it is our duty and our delight to press on to maturity. I pray this passage is written as an incentive and help to press on to the holi- ness without which we will not see the Lord. "Not that I have already attained, but one thing I do, forgetting those things which are behind and reaching forward to those things which are ahead." It's the phrase, "forgetting those things which are behind" that I want to write about as I close the book. There are a lot of problems associated with forgetting the past. Some will say it is impossible to forget the past.

Why consider it at all? Because it is a possible task to attain; and because of the benefits and blessing we will receive by doing it. It is important to understand at the outset that when Paul talks about forgetting the past he is not referring to erasing the past. Those of you who are familiar with how a computer handles the information that we imput into its memory know that there is a "delete" key that is used to remove information we don't want stored in the computer. To some, "delete" means to remove permanently as if it was erased, completely purged. This doesn't happen. When a person hits the "delete" key the information disappears from the screen but it is still in the computer's memory.

Although it has been deleted it may still be found. The information is not erased or permanently and irrecoverably gone. It can be recovered. We cannot erase our past. This does not mean we cannot forget the past in the sense that Paul had in mind. What is Paul saying when he tells us to forget the things that in the past? In the text, Paul is encouraging us to break out of the hostage situation. He is saying don't allow the past to hold you in bondage. I thank God that He was in the mist of all of my mess. He has shown me what the Lord can do. Don't be a prisoner of your past. Past blunders, mistakes, failures and hurts need not have a stranglehold on your life. Some people will even put you on a guilt trip. Make up your mind to be happy – learn to find pleasure in simple things. Make the best of circumstances. No one has everything, and everyone has something of sorrow. Don't take yourself too seriously.

Don't let criticism worry you because you can't please everybody. Don't let your neighbors set your standard – be yourself. Do things you enjoy doing, but stay out of debt. Don't borrow trouble. Imaginary things are harder to bear than actual ones. Avoid people who make you unhappy.

Don't spend time brooding over sorrows and mistakes. Keep busy at something. A very busy person never has time to be unhappy. Why is it important to forget those things that are behind? Looking back encourages the possibility of going back. It was so with Lot's wife. God's message to Lot and his wife were clear: "Escape for your life! Do not look behind you…" (Gen. 19:17 NKJV). I have tried to be as positive as possible, about – facing the challenge of forget- ting the things that are past. I have tried to say we do not have to be held in bondage by our past. There is hope for deliverance. There is hope for change. There is hope for closing the door on the past that made you a hostage; a victim instead of a victor. Not that I have already obtained this, but I press on to make it my own because Christ Jesus has made me his own. Beloved, I do not consider that I have made it my own; but this one thing I do; forgetting what lies behind and straining forward to what lies ahead, I press on toward the goal for the prize of the heavenly call of God in Christ Jesus. Life is a journey. In several places in his writings, Paul compares life and the faith to a race; a race in which we need great endurance. I've always liked that analogy but once I've come to appreciate even more is the image of life as a journey. A race is a one time event, short lived, and then it's over until another race is orga- nized. Journeys, on the other hand, can be brief or they can be long. A race has a finish line, while a journey has a destination. A race has one purpose, to win. The purpose of a journey is arriving at the destination but part of the joy of the journey is the adventure and the stops along the way. So let's think about life as an ongoing journey of faith; road- blocks and speed bumps. But into every journey there usually come a few roadblocks, detours and speed bumps. Sometimes the vehicle even breaks down and we have to take it into the repair shop. In every journey, there is a lot of joy but usually there is also some disappointment and even some pain and sorrow. They frustrate us like roadblocks, detours and speed bumps. They tempt us to give up. Press on and look what the Lord can do. The apostle Paul tells us not to give up and not to quit. He uses himself as an exam- ple. As Paul addresses the Philippians, he is speaking words of encouragement. He is helping them and encouraging them not to give up, but to press on. Jesus does the same thing for us in our journey of life. Through the Holy Spirit, through the work of the church and through our disciple- ship, we are encouraged to press on. One of the ways we press on is through prayer. In our journey through life, we too are off course a lot of time. For some people, it is most of the time. But by staying in constant contact with God through prayer, we can correct our course. We can stay headed in the right direction. The navigator (Jesus) can get us to our destination despite the roadblocks, detours and flat tires. Another way to press on and be encouraged is through regular worship. Find a good church and worship with other Christians and watch what God can do. In worship, we meet the Savior and we hear words of encour- agement. In worship, we gather with others and are sup- ported and encouraged through their presence and through their words of encouragement. Through worship, we find rest. God created the Sabbath as a day of rest, a day to refocus our lives on God and reevaluate our priorities.

Another aspect of pressing on is the need to stop and refuel.Prayer, worship, Sunday school and personal bible study are all excellent ways to refuel and be fed. But the best, of course, is Holy

Communion. He will meet you, feed you, and encourage you to press on and continue in this journey of life, pursing the prize. Paul says, "I press on toward the goal for the prize of the upward call of God in Christ Jesus." Paul says, "I pursue the Prize, I press toward the goal." We have noted all along that the prize and the goal is the same thing: it is like Jesus Christ. That was the single focus of Paul's life. Back in verse 8 of Philippians 3, he says, "I count everything else to be loss, I have one great quest, to know Christ Jesus my Lord: He says in verse 13, "One thing I do, and that one thing is forgetting the other things, I press on toward the goal." So he had a life focus of knowing Jesus Christ so well, so deeply, so richly that he was becoming like Christ. That is the goal of every Christian's life. The goal of my life is to be like Christ. Everything else spins off of that. God has been good to me and I owe it all to Him. All my service, all my relationships, all my worship, everything spins off of being like Christ. If I am like Christ, I will worship God in the way He worshipped God. If I am like Christ I will serve God in the way He served God. If I am like Christ, I will relate to people in the love in which He related to people. In other words, the simple focus of my life is to be like Christ. That is why I must let the word about Christ dwell in me richly. That is why if 1 John 2:6 says: "I abide in Him. I must walk the way He walked." If I'm to be like Christ, this is the goal of my life. So the goal of my life as a Christian is outside of me, it is not in me, it is outside of me, it is beyond me. I am not preoccupied with myself; I am preoccupied with becoming like Christ. That is some- thing that only the Holy Spirit can do as I focus on Christ. I focus on Him and the Spirit transforms me into His image. Now in the Christian life, we are pressing toward a goal.

That goal is not the satisfaction of my own desire of greater significance. That is not the goal of my life. The goal of my life is to be like Christ. Thus, I press on to say: Look what the Lord can do if you only trust Him. Thank God for what he has done and doing in my life.

Chapter Seven: Press On

Chapter 8:

Your Time Has Come

This is your time of healing. Your appointed time to be blessed is now. This last chapter is for those who are questioning when is God going to fulfill His promise upon their life as he has mine. Can I declare to you that your testimony is now and it is the right time for you to be blessed? There is nothing you can do if your time has not come. There is a time for every thing, but your time has come. In the book of John 5:1-11, Jesus was at the pool of Bethesda means a place or house of mercy. There, Jesus had mercy upon a man whose time had come. I declare to you today that where you are, if you allow Jesus to come in, He will make your house (body) a house of mercy. I believe someone is going to experience the mercy of God today.

Shout – your time has come. Psalms 102:13 said the set time to favor you has come and it is now. It is your time to be blessed, delivered, favored and free and to receive liberty. The bible in John 5 taught me God would come where I was and that he did. You don't have to go anywhere to get your mercy or healing. Some of us focus our faith and attention on the occasional stirring of the water. It is time to focus on Jesus. The man had been focusing on the water. He was at the house of mercy but he did not receive mercy because his time had not yet come. Some of us have been in our disability for years, but it is your time now. You've seen people blessed, but it is your time. Verse 5 states: "And a certain man was there, which had an infirmity thirty and eight years." One thing is clear of the man; he may not have received his mercy for 38 years but he did not move out of the house of mercy. Stay in the house of mercy, stay in the house of God. The power of the Lord is there where you are. His glory is in the house. Don't allow people to deceive you and push you away. He stayed for 38 years. Stay and see the glory of God. He will take you to a new dimension. The time to favor Zion is now – Hallelujah! I had been at my pool of sickness for 26 years, "Look What God can do". This man had been there for 38 years, I'm glad I didn't have to beat his record. He didn't know how to get out of disability, but he stayed there. You might not know how to get out of your limitation, barrenness, sickness, debt, sorrow or lone- liness but I've got news for you your time has come! Jesus bypassed a lot of people that day to get to the man whose time had come. The man was at the house of mercy but still lacking. The only thing that is missing is the Great Healer, but the Great Healer will come in if you let Him. Jesus said, "Do you want to be healed?" The man said I have no one.

Jesus said that you won't need anyone arise. The One with you now is Greater; and Greater is He that is in me than he that is in the world. The Great Healer is here! Your Redeem- er is here! Your Savior is here! The Great Provider is here!

Habakkuk 2:3 said if you want to receive your deliverance, "wait for it". The advice is wait. When all things are right and God's time has come, your deliverance will come. Do not quit. I am not quitting. I have waited too long to quit. What if that man quit after 10, 20, 30, 371/2, or 37 years, 11 months and 29 days? He would have died of his infirmity. People may laugh at you and say you are still where you were yesterday, but wait. People may step on you, but wait. People may say you still believe you can be pregnant after 20 years of marriage, but wait. The only people that win the race are those who never quit. I thank God after 26 years I didn't quit or give up. After five years of saying I was going to write a book. I couldn't quit. Praise God. Don't allow anyone to pull you out of God's house of mercy. When they try to push you out, be quick to let them know that it is your turn and it is your time to be blessed. Jacob knew that his time had come when he refused to let the angel go. The woman with the virtue of blood pressed on because she re- alized that this was her time and she had to take the oppor- tunity. I don't know whom I'm writing to or who is reading this book but your time has come. Are you ready now because: your time has come Praise the name of the Lord!

About Scott Gordon

Scott L. Gordon was born in Sapulpa, Oklahoma. He is a graduate of Sand Springs Public Schools; he also attend- ed Tulsa Vo-Tech and Oklahoma Junior College, Rhema Correspondence Bible School (Diploma), and Oklahoma School of Religion Langston (associate degree in Biblical Studies) (Bachelor of Arts in Pastoral Ministries) Master of Arts in Christian Education). He is married to Kristi

(Rider/ Blalock) Gordon, and they are the proud parents of Brandon, Nastosha and Taylor.

Scott was licensed and ordained by the late Reverend Ervin Ruth. Under his leadership, Scott held the office of Youth Minister for five years prior to becoming the Interim Pastor. Scott L. Gordon was called to pastor Calvary Baptist Church and Installation services were held on February 8, 2002. He believes that the church is a hospital and that everyone is welcomed to the spiritual, mental, financial and physical healing that only God can provide.

Scott does Missionary work in third world countries (Nicaragua, Ghana, Nairobi Kenya, and Dominican Republic). And London , Serve as a Hospice chaplain For past 13 years presently serve as Chaplain and family support for Miller Hospice, A member of National Baptist State Con- vention Inc. USA, Where he received his Pastor's Teaching Certificate, Southern Baptist and Full Gospel Baptist, One Church One Child, Hope Community Center, Has served as board member of Creek County Literacy Program, Big Brothers and Big Sisters of Oklahoma, Past President of Sapulpa Minister Alliance, past President of Tulsa Christian Together, and Youth Minister of the Canaan District Baptist Association. also served as a member of the International Fellowship of Christian Businessmen, Served as a board member of the T. Oscar Chappelle Oklahoma School of Religion, and Camp Loughridge; Scott L. Gordon delivered the first message for the First Annual Tulsa Together Youth Service. Although Scott is a busy steward, he also finds time for the Prison Ministry, serve, volunteers at Schools and Nursing Homes doing devotional for a group of young and elderly people, Past Owner of Gordon's tree and lawn ser- vice, CEO of 180 Realty LLC. and delivers weekly television broadcast on WWHB. President of Scott L Gordon Minis- tries Author of two books Own and CEO of SLG ROPERI- TY LLC. And 180 REALTY LLC

He is a dynamic, energetic, passionate, spirit-filled, loving, warm, caring and sharing person. He is a dreamer and a visionary. He can deliver God's message in his own unique and inspiring way.

www.ingramcontent.com/pod-product-compliance
Lightning Source LLC
Chambersburg PA
CBHW060402050426
42449CB00009B/1858